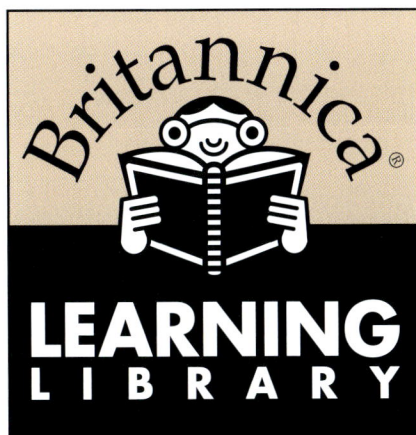

Familiar Animals

Get to know the animals that live closest to us

ENCYCLOPÆDIA
Britannica®

CHICAGO   LONDON   NEW DELHI   PARIS   SEOUL   SYDNEY   TAIPEI   TOKYO

I N T R O D U C T I O N

Do snakes chew their food? Why are donkeys called 'beasts of burden'? What insect might survive a nuclear bomb blast? Are pigs smart?

In *Familiar Animals,* you'll discover answers to these questions and many more. Through pictures, articles, and fun facts, you'll encounter amazing animals from around the world.

To help you on your journey, we've provided the following signposts in *Familiar Animals*:

■ **Subject Tabs**—The coloured box in the upper corner of each right-hand page will quickly tell you the article subject.

■ **Search Lights**—Try these mini-quizzes before and after you read the article and see how much - *and how quickly* - you can learn. You can even make this a game with a reading partner. (Answers are upside down at the bottom of one of the pages.)

■ **Did You Know?**—Check out these fun facts about the article subject. With these surprising 'factoids', you can entertain your friends, impress your teachers, and amaze your parents.

■ **Picture Captions**—Read the captions that go with the photos. They provide useful information about the article subject.

■ **Vocabulary**—New or difficult words are in **bold type**. You'll find them explained in the Glossary at the end of the book.

■ **Learn More!**—Follow these pointers to related articles in the book. These articles are listed in the Table of Contents and appear on the Subject Tabs.

Britannica®

LEARNING LIBRARY

Have a great trip!

A cracker butterfly rests on the leaf of a plant.
© George D. Lepp/Corbis

Familiar Animals

TABLE OF CONTENTS

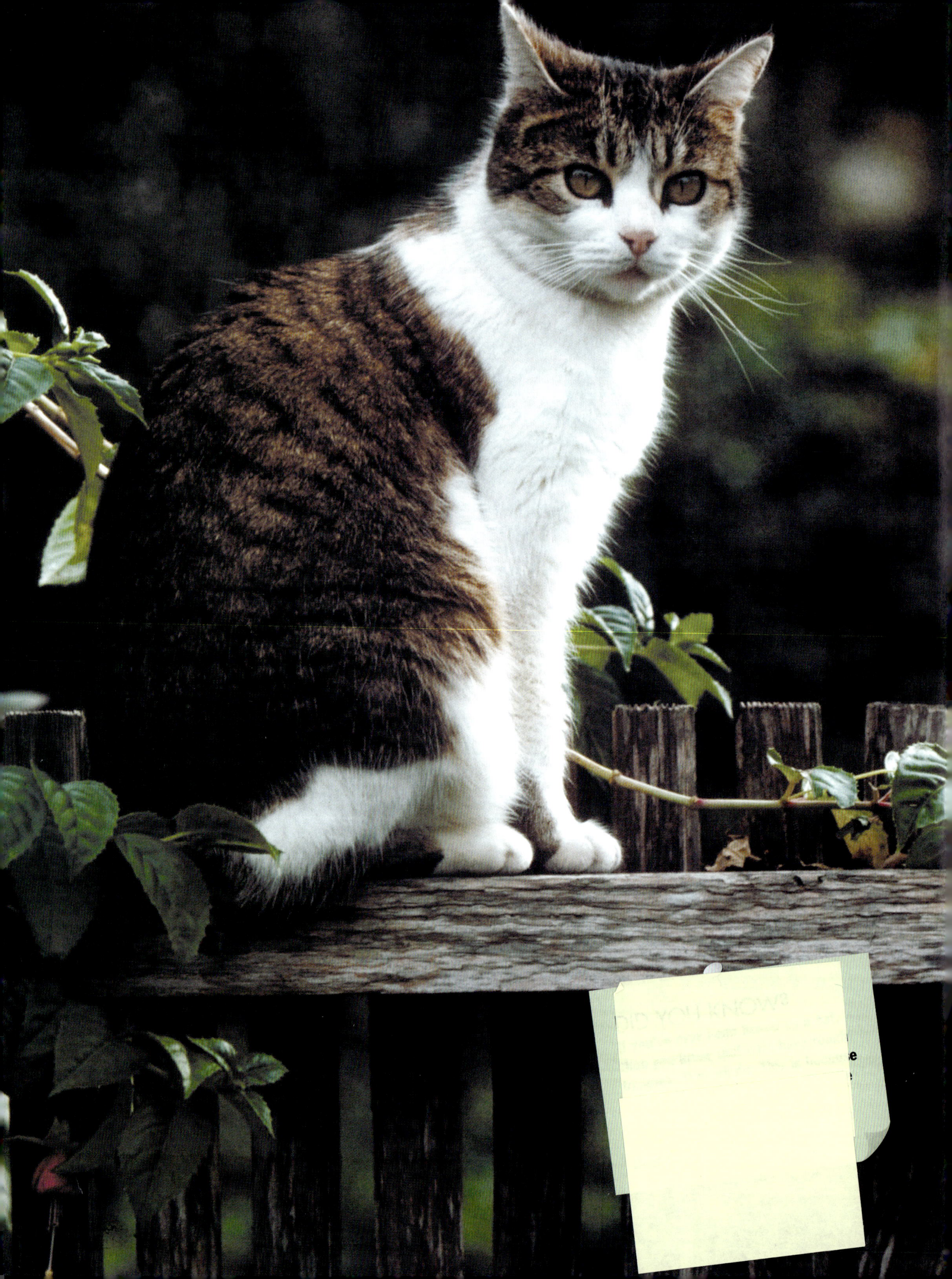
DID YOU KNOW?

The Tiger in Your House

If a cat lives with you, you have a member of a proud, sometimes fierce family as a pet. A tiger is a cat. So are lions, leopards, and cheetahs. Jaguars, lynx, panthers, and pumas are cats too.

All cats have five toes on their front paws and four on their back paws. They have long sharp claws. They use their claws for climbing trees, catching food, and protecting themselves against other animals. All cats except the cheetah can move their claws in and out.

Pet cat being cuddled.
© Jose Luis Pelaez, Inc./Corbis

All cats purr, making a low, continuous, rattling hum. The purr is a relaxing, self-comforting sound that can signal a friendly mood. Many cats also meow, though 'big cats' (such as lions and tigers) roar. Most cats don't like to go in water, but they can all swim if they have to. Cats can hear even faraway things. And they can see at night when it's very dark. They are also among the fastest animals on Earth. In fact, the cheetah can run faster than any other animal, but only for a short distance.

Though **domestic** cats are usually fed by their owners, cats naturally get their food by hunting. They'll eat anything from mice to zebras, depending on how big a cat they are. Some will eat fish, clams, and snails. When house cats play with string and small toys, they're displaying their ancient family hunting **instinct**.

Cats have existed on the Earth for a very long time. The people of Egypt were the first to keep cats as pets. They gave them milk in gold saucers and made statues of cats. When cats died, they were often buried in special graveyards or even made into mummies!

LEARN MORE! READ THESE ARTICLES...
BIRDS • DOGS • RABBITS AND HARES

The domestic cat (house cat) is one of the most popular house pets. In ancient Thailand, cats lived in kings' castles.
© Craig Lovell/Corbis

Answer: Both lions and house cats eat meat. They also both purr, have five toes on their front feet, and are very quick. But cats can live in your house. Lions are too big and too wild to be pets.

Most Valuable Creatures on Earth

In Iran they were sacrificed to the gods. In India they are treated as **sacred**. In the ancient world they were used as money. Almost everywhere they have been used as a source of milk, butter, cheese, and meat. Cattle have, for thousands of years, been humanity's most valuable animals.

The word 'cattle' once meant all kinds of domestic animals. It comes from the Latin word *capitale*, which means 'wealth' or 'property'. The word 'cattle' is used now only for certain **bovines**, the animal group that includes oxen, bison, and buffalo.

A bull is a male bovine and a cow is a female - though the term 'cow' is often used for both. A calf is the young of either sex. Cattle that are between 1 and 2 years old are called 'yearlings'. The natural lifespan of cattle is about 20 years, but most of them are sent to slaughter long before they reach this age.

Today's domestic cattle in Africa, Asia, and Indonesia are very much like the cattle that lived in those areas 2,000 years ago. In Europe and America, however, cattle farmers have produced new breeds. Nowadays cattle are classified as dairy, beef, or **dual**-purpose types, which means they are used for both dairy and beef production.

One of the most popular breeds of cattle is the Brown Swiss breed. It is classified as a dairy cow in the United States and as a dual-purpose type in other countries. It may be one of the oldest breeds of cattle. A grown Brown Swiss cow weighs about 680 kilos. Other popular breeds include the Guernsey, the Jersey, and the Holstein.

© Hans Georg Roth/Corbis

© Royalty-Free/Corbis

(Top) Cows at a livestock market.
(Bottom) Longhorn resting under a tree.

SEARCH LIGHT

Fill in the gaps:
A _____ is a male bovine and a _____ is a female.

LEARN MORE! READ THESE ARTICLES...
HORSES • PIGS • SHEEP

Cattle have served many purposes to human beings over the years. Holstein cows such as these can be a source of dairy products.

© Gunter Marx Photography/Corbis

DID YOU KNOW?
Cattle are ruminants - animals that bring their food back up after it has been swallowed, to be rechewed and reswallowed. This process is known as 'chewing the cud'.

Dogs, some of the most popular animals in the world, come in many shapes and sizes. They were among the first animals to be domesticated, or tamed, by humans.

© Tim Davis/Corbis

The Loyal Companions

For thousands of years, dogs have held a special place in people's hearts. They are known as 'man's best friend'. This is because they are so brave, loving, and loyal. Dogs are used to living in groups called 'packs' and obeying the pack leader. Now humans are their pack leaders. Dogs depend on people for food - mostly meat - and perform services in return.

Since prehistoric times, dogs have worked for people. They have tracked game animals and retrieved them on land and water, guarded

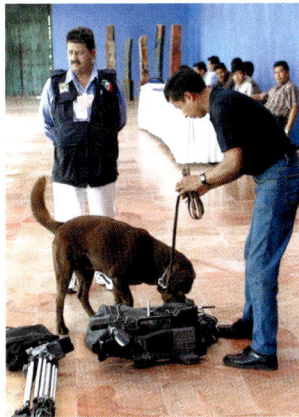

Security guard with police dog examining bags at a convention in Mexico.
© AFP/Corbis

houses, and pulled sledges. They have delivered messages, herded sheep, and even rescued people trapped in snow. They sniff out illegal drugs and explosives, help police make arrests, and guide visually impaired people. Fast-running dogs are also used in races.

Dogs have many abilities and characteristics that make them useful. Sharp teeth are one of these. Most dogs can smell fainter odours and hear higher notes than any person. And although dogs don't see many colours, they are very good at noticing movement.

Dogs come in many shapes, sizes, and **temperaments**. A big Irish wolfhound stands about 80 centimetres high at the withers, or top of the shoulders. The chihuahua, however, stands about 13 centimetres tall. Herding dogs such as collies tend to be intelligent. Terriers, which were bred to catch rodents, were originally quite fierce. But many different breeds of dogs now make playful family pets.

Dogs have been **domesticated** for much of human history. When Pompeii - the ancient Italian city that was buried by a volcano in AD 79 - was excavated, a dog was found lying across a child. Apparently it was trying to protect the child.

LEARN MORE! READ THESE ARTICLES…
CATS • COYOTES • HORSES

Answer: On average, the difference between the Irish wolfhound and the chihuahua is 69 centimetres.

11

Beasts of Burden

SEARCH LIGHT

What's one way that donkeys are like horses? What's one way that they're different?

Donkeys were among the first animals to be tamed by humans. The first donkeys probably came from Asia. People ride donkeys and use them to carry heavy loads, or **burdens**. Because they are surefooted, donkeys are useful on rough or hilly ground.

Donkeys play an important part in the lives of people in the mountains of Ethiopia and other parts of north-eastern Africa. They are also important to the people in the high plains of Tibet and in parts of South America.

Donkeys can be found in a range of sizes. From the ground to the shoulder, the American donkey can be 168 centimetres tall, while the Sicilian donkey is only about 81 centimetres tall. The donkey's long ears are its most noticeable feature. Donkeys are usually white, grey, or black in colour, or shades in between. Most of them have a dark stripe from their mane to their tail. The mane of a donkey is short and tends to stick out.

Donkey carries load through the streets of Colombia, South America.
© Jeremy Horner/Corbis

Donkeys can survive on almost any kind of plant for food, but usually they eat hay or grass. They are gentle and patient and become fond of their masters if they are treated well. This is why some people prefer donkeys to horses or mules.

The donkey is related to the horse. Sometimes people **crossbreed** a donkey with a horse. When the father is a donkey and the mother is a horse, the baby is called a 'mule'. Another name for a donkey is a burro, which is the Spanish word for the animal.

LEARN MORE! READ THESE ARTICLES...
CATTLE • HORSES • SHEEP

This donkey shows how important these animals can be to their owners. Donkeys are gentle and patient and become fond of their masters if they are treated kindly.

© Galen Rowell/Corbis

DID YOU KNOW?
Donkeys can be famously stubborn. If they don't want to move, then no amount of pushing or pulling will budge them.

Answer: Donkeys and horses look very much alike, with similar faces, legs, bodies, tails, and manes. Horses, however, are generally much taller than donkeys. And donkeys are generally considered better pack animals and are more patient than horses.

Strong and Graceful Animal Friends

The horse has been a friend to human beings for thousands of years. Long ago, horses were used to carry soldiers onto the battlefield. They have also pulled carriages, carts, and heavy farm machinery. Today people ride horses and use them for hunting, playing **polo**, and racing. Horses even perform in circuses.

A herd of galloping horses in New Zealand.
© Kit Houghton/Corbis

The reason horses have been used in so many ways is because they are large and strong. A typical horse weighs more than 450 kilos! It can stand more than 1.5 metres tall at the shoulder. From its nose to its tail, it's about 2.7 metres long.

The legs of a horse are strong even though they look very slender. When a horse is moving, its back legs give it the power to move forward and its front legs give it support.

A horse's foot is really just one large toe, and the hoof is like a thick toenail. The part of the hoof that can be seen when the horse's feet are on the ground is called the 'wall'. A horseshoe is fitted to the underside of the wall to protect it from cracking.

A horse's eyes are larger than those of any other land animal. But horses have a problem with sight. A horse sees things first with one eye and then with the other. So even small **stationary** objects appear to move. This frightens the horse. To keep a horse calm, the owner sometimes fits pads called 'blinders', or 'blinkers', on the outer sides of the eyes. This prevents the horse from seeing things that might frighten it.

LEARN MORE! READ THESE ARTICLES...
CATTLE • DOGS • DONKEYS

SEARCH LIGHT

Fill in the gap: The outside part of a horse's hoof is called the '_____'.

14

Many people still enjoy horseback riding. This woman is riding seated in what's called a 'stock saddle'. American ranchers and cowboys developed this comfortable seat. The more formal 'English saddle' is used with many show horses.
© Royalty-Free/Corbis

Answer: The outside part of a horse's hoof is called the 'wall'.

Smarties with Dirty Faces

Did you know that in tests of intelligence, pigs have proved to be among the smartest of all domestic animals - even more intelligent than dogs?

The world's largest population of **domestic** pigs is in China. The second largest population of domestic pigs is in the United States, and the third largest is found in Brazil.

Besides domestic pigs, there are several species of wild pigs found in Europe, Asia, and Africa. The **pygmy** hog is the smallest of the wild pigs. It is found in Nepal and northern India. It is now in danger of becoming extinct. The warty pig and the bearded pig live in parts of Southeast Asia, Malaysia, and the Philippines.

Wild pigs eat a wide variety of foods, including leaves, roots, fruit, and reptiles. Food for domestic pigs includes maize and other grains, and some kinds of rubbish too. A pig's snout ends in a flat rounded disk. Pigs use their snouts to search for food. Both male and female wild pigs have **tusks** on their snouts, which they use for defence.

A female pig is old enough to have piglets when she is about a year old. Before she gives birth to her first **litter**, the female pig is known as a 'gilt'. After the first litter, she is known as a 'sow'. Sows can have as many as 20 piglets in a litter, but a litter of 10 or 11 is the average. A male pig is called a 'boar'. A young **weaned** pig of either sex is called a 'shoat'.

(Top) Pigs enjoying a mud bath; (bottom) getting friendly with a piglet.

© Eye Ubiquitous/Corbis

© Julie Habel/Corbis

LEARN MORE! READ THESE ARTICLES…
CATTLE • HORSES • SHEEP

DID YOU KNOW?
People think pigs are dirty animals because they so often see pigs wallowing in mud. But pigs cover themselves with mud to stay cool. Given a choice, pigs prefer air-conditioning to mud baths.

Find and correct the mistake in the following sentence: Pigs have proved to be among the least smart of all domestic animals.

Female pigs can have as many as 20 piglets in a litter. China holds the record for having the largest population of domestic pigs. The United States is second.

Answer: Pigs have proved to be among the smartest of all domestic animals.

DID YOU KNOW?
Some breeds of horned sheep may grow more than one pair of horns. For example, Jacob sheep, a British breed that is also raised in the United States, may grow as many as three pairs of horns.

Follow the Leader

Like Mary's little lamb, sheep like to follow a leader, usually an old ram (male sheep). They live together in groups called 'flocks'. If the shepherd or farmer who takes care of the sheep can get the leader going in the right direction, the rest will follow. Sometimes well-trained and specially reared dogs called 'sheepdogs' help herd the sheep and keep them from getting lost.

Domestic sheep are very useful animals. Their thick, soft fleece, or wool, is used for making clothes and blankets. Some sheep are raised for their meat. In many countries people drink sheep's milk, which is also used for making cheese.

A sheep's wool is cut off with **shears**, much as your hair is trimmed with scissors. Sheep are sheared only once a year, at a time when they won't be too cold without their wool. Sheep do something else that people do: they take baths. They are herded into tanks of water with chemicals in it. This mixture of chemicals and water is called a 'sheep-dip', and it is used to protect the sheep from **parasites**. Sheep also have to have shots from a **veterinarian**.

(Top) Dall's sheep, a variety found in Alaska; (bottom) a boy holds a fleecy lamb (young sheep).

Did you know that sheep are easily scared? Even a sheet of paper blowing in the wind will frighten them. Thunderstorms also frighten them.

There are wild sheep in many parts of the world. They look a lot like goats, but there are some ways to tell the two apart. Sheep don't have beards, for example, but many goats do. Also, sheep's horns curl around the sides of their heads, but goats' horns arch toward the backs of their heads.

LEARN MORE! READ THESE ARTICLES...
CATTLE · DOGS · PIGS

SEARCH LIGHT

Which of the following is *not* a feature that sheep and goats share?
a) giving milk
b) growing a beard
c) producing wool

Sheep are raised all over the world. This shepherd in Chile leads his sheep down a mountain road.
© Galen Rowell/Corbis

Answer: b) growing a beard

What
do birds
have that no
other animal has?

DID YOU KNOW?
A few birds have a curious trick of stroking their feathers with live ants. It's not clear why they do this. One explanation is that an acid produced by the ants seems to kill or drive away insects.

Birds of a Feather

Like many animals, birds are **warm-blooded**. They have many other features in common with other animals, too. But they have one feature that makes them **unique** among all living animals: birds have feathers.

The entire covering of feathers is called the bird's 'plumage'. Feathers are an important part of why most birds can fly. And feathers help protect all birds from rain, cold, and heat.

The next time it rains, watch for birds outside the window. You may see them standing with wings and tail drooping to the ground. The water simply slides off without soaking through. On a cold winter day you may notice that birds fluff out their feathers. Fluffed-out feathers hold a layer of warm air next to the skin. In hot weather a bird flattens its feathers. This keeps the skin cool by stopping hot air from reaching it.

Birds have different kinds of feathers. In many birds a thick coat of feathers called 'down' lies closest to the skin. Down feathers are soft and warm. Water birds have extra-thick coats of down. That's one reason why ducks can paddle about in icy winter waters without getting cold.

A bird's main body feathers are called '**contour** feathers'. Most contour feathers have many small hooks. The tiny hooks lock together like a zip, which makes the feathers smooth in a single direction. Some contour feathers are colourful and are for show only. Other contour feathers are special 'flight feathers'. These are found on the edges and tips of the wing and in the tail. They can be adjusted as a bird flies to help the bird steer and change speed.

LEARN MORE! READ THESE ARTICLES…
BUTTERFLIES AND MOTHS · INSECTS · LIZARDS

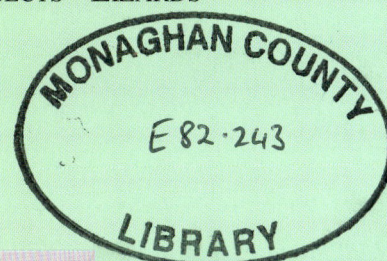

Answer: Birds are the only living animals to have feathers.

Riders of the Wind

If an eagle spread its wings in your room, it would take up as much space as your bed. Eagles have been called the 'king of birds' because of their **majestic** appearance and power of flight. They fly easily, using air currents to ride the wind.

Eagles are birds of prey, which means that they hunt other animals for food. One reason they are such good hunters is that they have excellent eyesight. Even when an eagle is so high in the air that it can hardly be seen, it can still see small objects on the ground. When it spots a meal, it swoops down and grabs the animal with its strong claws. Then it uses its hooked beak to tear the animal apart.

Golden eagle.
© Royalty-Free/Corbis

Eagles build huge nests of sticks on rocky cliffs or in the treetops. Their nests are big enough to hold people! Eagles use the same nest year after year, returning to it with the same mate.

When there are eggs to hatch, both the mother and the father eagles take turns sitting on them. Both parents care for the little eagles afterward, taking them mice, fish, rabbits, ducks, snakes, and squirrels to eat. But eagles don't always catch their own food. Sometimes they steal food from another bird by chasing the bird until it gets tired and drops whatever it is carrying.

Not all eagles look alike. A golden eagle has a cap of gold feathers on its head. A bald eagle is not really bald, but it looks that way because its head feathers are white and its body feathers are brown.

LEARN MORE! READ THESE ARTICLES…
BIRDS • KINGFISHERS • OWLS

DID YOU KNOW?

When eagles choose a mate, they do a dramatic high-flying act called cartwheeling. Gripping each other with their claws, they plunge together toward the ground. At the last moment they pull apart and fly upward again.

Near Kenai, Alaska, a bald eagle perches on a branch.
© Theo Allofs/Corbis

SEARCH LIGHT

Find and correct the error in the following sentence: Only female eagles take care of the babies.

Answer: Both male and female eagles take care of the babies.

SEARCH LIGHT

Find and correct the error in the following sentence: The most commonly seen kingfisher in North America is the kookaburra.

Laugh, Kookaburra!

The birds known as kingfishers are found all over the world, but most kinds live in **tropical** areas. Many kingfishers are brightly coloured, especially the ones found in Southeast Asia. All are famous for their swift dives.

© Len Robinson—Frank Lane Picture Agency/Corbis

© Lanz Von Horsten—Gallo Images/Corbis

(Top) Sacred kingfisher; (bottom) Malachite kingfisher.

Kingfishers are often boldly patterned. Many of them have **crests** on their large heads. Their bodies are squat, and their bills are long and heavy. A kingfisher's long bill helps it to catch fish as it swoops into the water.

The most commonly spotted kingfisher in North America is the belted kingfisher. It ranges from Canada to the Gulf Coast. You can recognize the belted kingfisher by its shaggy black crest. It also has bluish grey feathers on the upper part of its body and white on the under part. Both the male and the female seem to be wearing a belt! The male kingfisher has a belt of grey breast feathers. The female has a chestnut coloured belt.

The belted kingfisher makes its nest in a hole that it digs in the ground close to streams and lakes. The nest is full of fish bones. The belted kingfisher eats only fish, which it catches. Once the fish has been caught, the kingfisher whacks it against a branch a few times and then eats it whole!

Some kingfishers live in forests rather than near water. Among the forest kingfishers is the well known kookaburra of Australia. It eats reptiles, including poisonous snakes. The kookaburra is sometimes called the '**bushman's** clock', because it is heard early in the morning and just after sunset. It has a loud laughing or **braying** voice.

LEARN MORE! READ THESE ARTICLES…
BIRDS • OWLS • PARROTS AND COCKATOOS

DID YOU KNOW?

A pair of belted kingfishers will take turns digging a tunnel into a riverbank to create their nest. They dig with their bills and use their feet to kick the loose dirt from the tunnel's mouth.

Answer: The most commonly seen kingfisher in North America is the belted kingfisher.

25

DID YOU KNOW?
Owls swallow their food whole, and then afterward they cough up hard balls of the parts they can't eat, such as bones and fur. If you find these hairy lumps scattered under a tree, it's a pretty good bet there's an owl nearby.

The Nighttime Hunters

Maybe it's because they fly mostly at night that owls seem so mysterious. Some **superstitions** connect them with scary things such as witches. But owls aren't that mysterious, and they aren't scary. They are simply **nocturnal** birds. And they are very helpful to people.

Saw-whet owls.
Ron Austing—Frank Lane Picture Agency/Corbis

Owls are hunters. Some owls eat insects or fish, but most eat rodents, such as mice and rats. Without owls, there would be too many rodents, and rodents are serious **pests.**

Owls can see better at night than most animals. They have excellent hearing and can detect the smallest scratchings of a mouse. When it comes to locating **prey**, their hearing helps them more than their eyesight. Because of their soft feathers, owls fly silently and almost always surprise their prey. Owls catch their prey in their long strong claws and swallow it without chewing.

The only way an owl can look around is to turn its head. It can turn its head almost all the way around, turning it so fast that you can hardly see it move. Sometimes it looks as though the owl is turning its head all the way around in a full circle!

Some people say owls are wise. That is because they were once associated with Athena, the Greek goddess of wisdom.

Owls sleep during the day, hidden among tree branches. If you were to see an owl, you'd probably mistake it for a piece of bark. It would sit still, not moving a feather. It wouldn't even move its eyes. It couldn't, because an owl's eyes can't move! This is why owls seem to stare at you - if you're lucky enough to see one!

LEARN MORE! READ THESE ARTICLES…
BIRDS · EAGLES · INSECTS

SEARCH LIGHT

Why do some people think that owls can turn their heads all the way around in a circle?

Common barn owls live all over the world, except in Antarctica and Micronesia.
© Eric and David Hosking/Corbis

Answer: Owls can turn their heads to the left or the right almost all the way around. It's because the head snaps back so quickly, truly in the blink of an eye, that people think owls can turn their heads all the way around.

Bright Colours and Brilliant Whites

Parrots and cockatoos have long fascinated humans. These lively birds not only are beautiful but they entertain us with their chatter and behaviour as well. Many parrots are brightly coloured, with green feathers and patches of red, orange, or blue. Most cockatoos are white, and all have a patch of long feathers called a 'crest' on their head that stands up straight when the bird is excited.

Citron-crested cockatoo.
© Eric and David Hosking/Corbis

Parrots and cockatoos belong to the same family as cockatiels, macaws, parakeets, and many other colourful birds. The tiniest parrot is the pygmy parrot, which is only 7 centimetres long. The largest member of the family is a type of macaw that can be as much as 101 centimetres long.

All the birds in this family have strong hooked bills that can crack open nuts. Their thick fleshy tongues help them eat. Some birds have brush-tipped tongues that are useful in sucking **nectar** from flowers and juice from fruits.

Parrots and cockatoos have unusual feet. Two toes point forward and two point backward. This lets them climb trees swiftly and grasp their food firmly as they eat it. The birds can also use their strong bills to help them climb.

Parrots and cockatoos are found in most **tropical** regions of the world, especially in rainforests. These birds can live for 30 to 50 years. Some have been known to live for 80 years!

Some parrots talk, sing, laugh, and whistle. They have a sharp sense of hearing and can **echo** human sounds and speech. Cockatoos can talk too. They are very **impish** and like to play tricks - like figuring out how to escape from their cages!

SEARCH LIGHT

Fill in the gaps: Parrots and cockatoos have unusual feet, with _____ pointing forward and _____ pointing backward.

LEARN MORE! READ THESE ARTICLES…
BIRDS • KINGFISHERS • PEACOCKS

Macaws gather at Manu National Park in Peru to eat clay. The clay adds minerals to the birds' diet.
© Michael & Patricia Fogden/Corbis

DID YOU KNOW?

Like many rainforest animals, wild parrots are endangered. This is partly because their homes are destroyed when the forest is cut down or burned. But they are also threatened by people who hunt them in order to sell them as pets.

Answer: Parrots and cockatoos have unusual feet, with two toes pointing forward and two toes pointing backward.

Proud Birds

A peacock's feathers are brilliant shades of bronze, blue, green, and gold. It even has a little crown of feathers, called a 'crest', on the top of its head. The centre of attraction, though, is the peacock's long tail. At the tip of each tail feather is a big shiny spot ringed with blue and bronze that looks like an eye.

When the male peacock wants to attract a female peacock (called a 'peahen'), it dances! And again the action is all in the tail. The peacock lifts its tail and spreads it out like a fan. Every feather is shown off this way. At the end of this show, the peacock makes its tail feathers **vibrate**. This makes the quills in the long tail feathers rattle and rustle. The peahen is charmed!

Peahens do not have long tails or crests. They are green and brown in colour and almost as big as the males.

Peacocks live in the wild in Southeast Asia and belong to the pheasant family. Two important kinds of peacock are the green, or Javanese, peacock and the blue, or Indian, peacock. The green peacock is found from Myanmar to Java. The blue is found in India and Sri Lanka. These beautiful birds can also be seen in zoos around the world.

A long time ago, people kept peacocks at home. The ancient Greeks called the peacock 'Hera's bird'. In their religion, Hera was the wife of Zeus, the god of sky and weather. She was thought of as the queen of heaven. According to an old story, the eyelike markings on peacock feathers were the 100 eyes of the giant Argus.

LEARN MORE! READ THESE ARTICLES...
BIRDS • KINGFISHERS • PARROTS AND COCKATOOS

SEARCH LIGHT

The male peacock in the picture is spreading his tail feathers to try to
a) scare the peahen.
b) attract the peahen.
c) hide the peahen.

The male peacock displays his feathers to get the attention of the female.
© Terry W. Eggers/Corbis

DID YOU KNOW?
Peacocks may be beautiful birds, but they definitely don't have beautiful voices. Peacocks make a harsh screeching when they 'sing', if you can call it that.

Answer: b) attract the peahen.

The World's Largest Population

The Earth is home to more insects than any other kind of animal. Insects are unique among all creatures because their bodies are divided into three parts - the head, the thorax, and the abdomen. The head contains the mouth, the eyes, and the **antennas**. Some insects use their antennas for smelling. The thorax is similar to a person's chest. If an insect has wings, they are attached to the thorax. And some insects have ears on the thorax. The abdomen contains a large part of the **digestive system**.

Instead of having bones, insects have an outer covering to support the body. The muscles are attached to this covering. The outer layer of the covering is waxy and **waterproof**.

All insects have six legs. Their legs, like their wings, are attached to the thorax. Each leg has five different bending places. It's like having five knees.

Each kind of insect has features that help it get along in the world. The pond skater has little cups on its feet so that it can walk on water. Dragonflies can hover and turn in the air like little helicopters. They even look like helicopters!

Some insects make sounds like music. Perhaps the most beautiful music is made by the snowy tree cricket. This insect uses one of its front wings as a fiddle and the other as a bow. Locusts have two tiny shell-like drums close to their wings. When the wings flap, these drums sound like fingers tapping on a metal lid. Grasshoppers make sounds by rubbing their wings or their back legs together. In some places people keep crickets or grasshoppers in cages to listen to their songs.

LEARN MORE! READ THESE ARTICLES...
CRICKETS · GRASSHOPPERS · MOSQUITOES

DID YOU KNOW?
It may seem hard to believe, but in the countryside almost all the noises you hear at night are made by insects and frogs - even the ones that sound like birds or people.

SEARCH LIGHT

What
are the
three parts of
an insect's body?

Answer: The three parts of an insect's body are the head, the thorax, and the abdomen.

Two leafcutting ants are hard at work clipping out pieces of a leaf in a rainforest in Costa Rica. The fragments are transported to an underground nest that can include over 1,000 chambers and house millions of individual ants. The ants physically and chemically create 'gardens' of fungus that grow on the chewed leaves. The fungus then provides them with food.
© Steve Kaufman/Corbis

Insect
Castle Builders!

Most ants live in nests that they build in protected places. Many live underground, sometimes under a rock. Some ants live in trees or inside wild plants. Others build their nests on the ground, using tiny sticks, sand, mud, gravel, and even leaves.

An ant hill is a mound of sand or dirt where thousands of ants live and work. Inside the hill are special rooms where food is kept and other rooms for baby ants. Tunnels connect the rooms. Worker ants build the nest, make tunnels, and repair any damage to the ant hill.

Soldier ants guard the ant hill day and night and protect it from enemies. An ant has long feelers, called antennas, that stick out from its head. It can give messages to other ants by tapping them with its antennas. Ants smell with their antennas too. They use scents to tell whether another ant is a friend or an enemy. If an ant from another nest wanders into the ant hill, the soldiers will attack it. Deadly wars are often fought between two nests of ants.

The whole nest is ruled by the queen ant, the mother of all the ants. The queen lays her eggs in a special room in the ant hill, while the other ants feed, clean, and protect her.

The 'ant castle' doesn't have a barn or a stable. But in one room certain kinds of ants keep aphids, which are tiny green insects. Aphids are called 'ant cows' because the ants 'milk' them to get a sweet juice the aphids produce. Other ants are like farmers too. They grow fungus inside their nests, and the fungus is all they eat!

Large ant hill in the Northern Territory of Australia.
© Penny Tweedie/Corbis

SEARCH LIGHT

Why do you think ants touch feelers whenever they meet? (Hint: What important function do the feelers, or antennas, serve?)

LEARN MORE! READ THESE ARTICLES…
BEES • INSECTS • MOSQUITOES

Answer: Ants touch when they meet because that's how they communicate with one another. They also use their feelers to tell if an ant is an enemy or a friend.

35

SEARCH LIGHT

True or false? Drones have stingers.

Inside the Hive

Inside a honeybee hive you'll see bees. But you'll also see hundreds of little six-sided rooms, or 'cells'. The bees build these cells with a wax - beeswax - that they make inside their bodies.

The bees store many things in the wax cells, including honey, **nectar**, and a food called 'bee bread'. Bee bread is made of flower **pollen** mixed with honey. The cells are also used to hold the tiny eggs that will hatch into baby bees.

A bee pollinates a flower.
© George D. Lepp/Corbis

Most of the bees' work is done in spring and summer. That's when the honey is made and stored and when the queen bee lays most of her eggs. The queen bee is the biggest bee in the hive.

There are two other kinds of bee in the hive: drones and workers. Drones are larger than the workers and have no stingers. They don't do any work, but one drone mates with the queen and is the father of all the hive's workers.

Each of the worker bees has a special job. Some build the cells in the hive, and others keep the hive clean. Some workers are soldiers that guard the hive and chase away any bees, wasps, and other insects that might try to steal the hive's honey.

Other worker bees fly out to visit flowers and blossoms. They take pollen and nectar back to the hive to make bee bread and honey. Some bees even stay by the door of the hive and flap their wings quickly to blow cool air through the hive.

DID YOU KNOW?
Bees can tell if an intruder has entered the hive because the intruder smells different. But one kind of moth has found a way to sneak into hives. It fakes the smell of the hive just long enough to get in and steal some honey.

LEARN MORE! READ THESE ARTICLES…
ANTS • BUTTERFLIES AND MOTHS • INSECTS

Bees go about their work on a man-made honeycomb.
© Lynda Richardson/Corbis

Answer: FALSE. Only worker bees and queens have stingers.

Fly by Day, Fly by Night

Butterflies and moths are found throughout the world, from deserts to hot jungles to high up in snowy mountains. You can see them on every continent except Antarctica.

Butterflies and moths are insects, and like all insects they have three pairs of legs. Their bodies are divided into three sections: head, **thorax**, and **abdomen**. On either side of the head is a large special eye. These eyes are able to detect the smallest movement. But they cannot see faraway things very clearly.

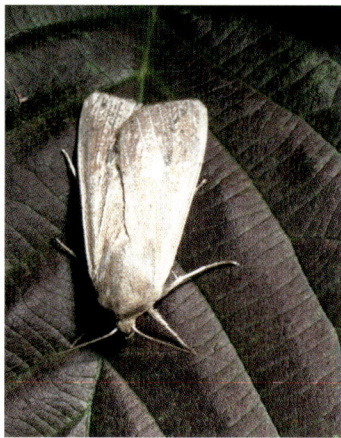

Brown moth.
© Karen Tweedy-Holmes/Corbis

The thorax, the middle section of the body, has two pairs of wings. The wings in front are usually larger. Dust-like scales cover the wings, body, and legs. If you happen to touch a butterfly or moth, these scales will come off in your hand.

If you want to know whether you are looking at a butterfly or a moth, you should look at its **antennae.** Butterflies and moths use their antennae to hear and smell. Butterfly antennae end in little round knobs. Moth antennae may look like tiny feathers or threads.

The most striking thing about butterflies is their colouring. Most are bright and beautiful. But most moths are dull coloured, with thicker bodies and smaller wings. Butterflies hold their wings straight up over their backs when they rest. Moths rest with their wings spread out. Butterflies are active during the day. But moths usually fly around at night.

Many butterflies and moths seem to like sweet things. **Nectar** from flowers is an important part of their diet. Some will eat mosses and ferns. Others like cones, fruits, and seeds, but some do not eat at all and live for only a short time!

LEARN MORE! READ THESE ARTICLES…
BEES · CRICKETS · INSECTS

SEARCH LIGHT

When do most butterflies fly, during the day or at night?

A cracker butterfly rests on the leaf of a plant.
© George D. Lepp/Corbis

Answer: Most butterflies fly during the day.

Cockroaches usually run and hide when a light is turned on in a dark room.

Indestructible Insects

Cockroaches have been around for many millions of years. This means that cockroaches lived through times when many other animals disappeared forever. They are very tough insects indeed. One type, the Oriental cockroach, can live for a month without food!

Cockroaches are found nearly everywhere. Some kinds live outside, but others live indoors alongside humans. These kinds are pests. They like warm dark areas in homes, offices, ships, trains, and even airplanes. Their broad flat bodies can squeeze through the narrowest of cracks. Although cockroaches may look like beetles, they are related to crickets. Like them, cockroaches use their long **antennae** on their heads for feeling through dark places.

Cockroaches usually hide during the day and come out at night to feed. They eat all sorts of plant and animal products, including paper, clothing, books, and other insects. Some cockroaches even eat other cockroaches.

Their feeding causes a lot of damage. And they have a nasty smell too. They can also cause allergies and are thought to spread diseases to humans. No wonder cockroaches are considered among the worst household pests.

Humans get rid of cockroaches with common poisons and traps. But cockroaches have many other enemies besides humans. Spiders, frogs, toads, lizards, and birds all feed on them.

There are more than 3,500 types of cockroach. Some are small, while others reach lengths of seven centimetres. Many are colourful. Most have two pairs of wings. Some, such as the American cockroach, can fly long distances. Others, such as the Oriental cockroach, can't fly at all. But all cockroaches have long powerful legs and can run very fast.

LEARN MORE! READ THESE ARTICLES…
CRICKETS • INSECTS • MOSQUITOES

SEARCH LIGHT

True or false? Most cockroaches hide at night and come out during the day.

DID YOU KNOW?
Many scientists believe that the cockroach is one of the few animals that could survive a nuclear bomb blast.

Answer: FALSE. Cockroaches usually hide during the day and come out at night to feed.

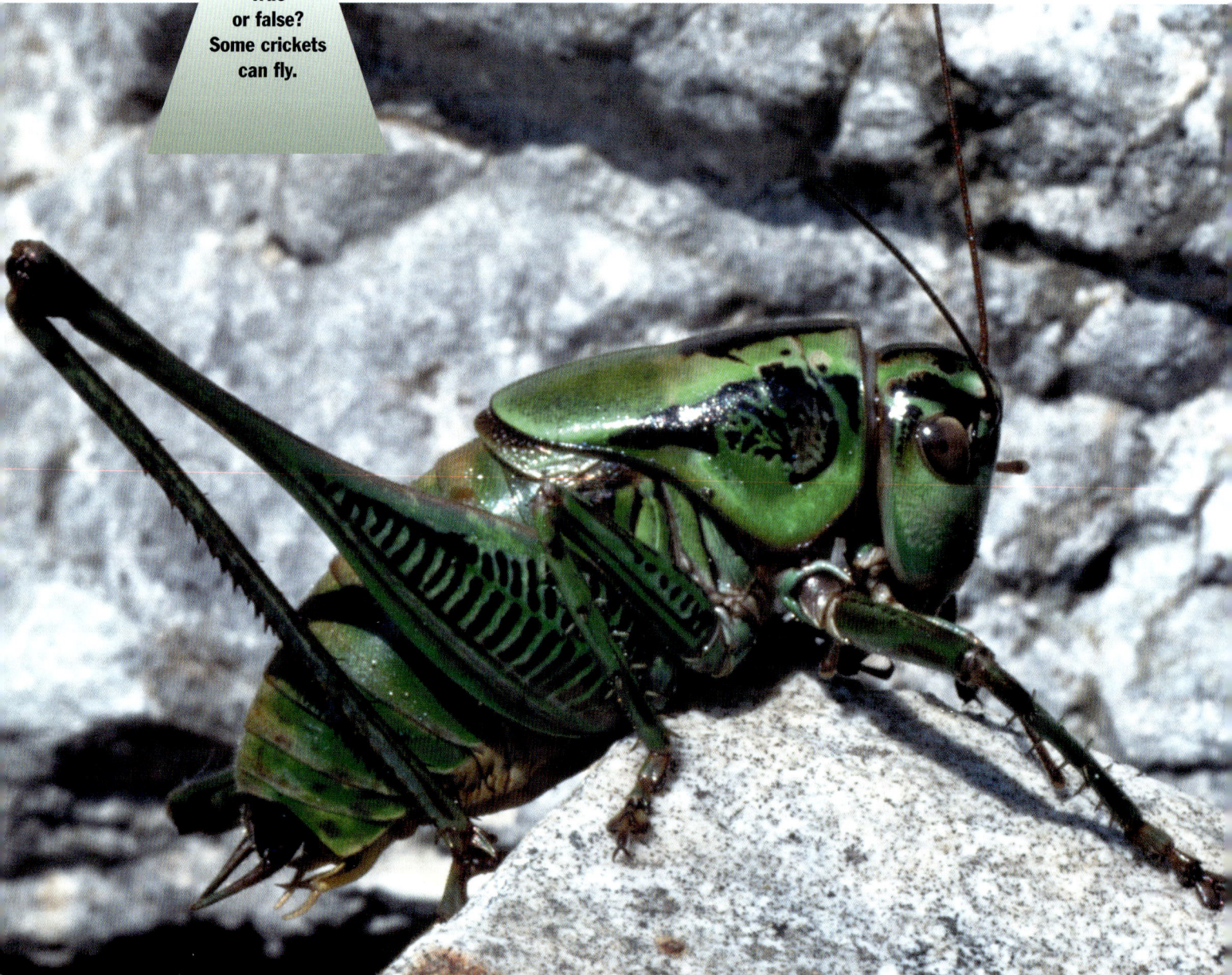

There are a number of myths about crickets. Some people
believe that harming a cricket will lead to bad luck.

The Wing Singers

A cricket never opens its mouth to chirp. Instead, it raises its stiff leathery front wings and rubs one over the other to make its high creaking sound. It's a loud noise for such a tiny insect. Some crickets are as small as your thumbnail.

Cricket on the head of a flower.
© Dennis Johnson—Papilio/Corbis

Only male crickets have music-making wings. The chirping lets female crickets know where to find them, and it also keeps other male crickets away. The smooth wings of female crickets make no sound. Some kinds of male and female crickets use their back wings for flying. But most crickets travel by hopping and jumping.

Some crickets eat only tiny insects. Others will eat almost anything. Crickets have such strong jaws that they can bite through clothes and even leather.

Like other insects, a cricket has six legs. On its feet there are tiny claws that help it dig or run along on a tree limb or ceiling. You'll never guess where a cricket's ears are. They're down near the joints of its front legs!

There are many different kinds of cricket. Crickets are black, green-brown, whitish, and straw coloured. There are the field crickets and brown house crickets. Both chirp during the day and night. But the white and green tree crickets and the bush crickets chirp only at night.

A special kind of cricket in North America is called a 'thermometer cricket'. Try counting how many times it chirps in 15 seconds and add 40 to it. Now you know the temperature in Fahrenheit degrees! The crickets chirp faster as the weather gets warmer.

LEARN MORE! READ THESE ARTICLES…
BUTTERFLIES AND MOTHS • GRASSHOPPERS • INSECTS

DID YOU KNOW?

Crickets are known to be such good 'singers' that they were once commonly kept in Chinese houses as pets.

Grasshoppers are green, olive, or brown and
may have yellow or red markings.
© Karl Switak—Gallo Images/Corbis

**Farmers
really don't like
some kinds of
grasshoppers.
What are these
grasshoppers called?**

Garden-Variety Hoppers

Grasshoppers are insects that are found all over the world. They live in all kinds of places but are most common in grasslands and tropical forests. One type spends most of its life on floating plants. But grasshoppers also live in people's gardens. Their brown or green colouring helps them blend in with the plants and soil around them.

Bladder grasshopper.
© Anthony Bannister—Gallo Images/Corbis

The reason grasshoppers are fond of gardens is that they are **vegetarians**. And people grow many things that grasshoppers like to eat. In some parts of the world, grasshoppers called locusts travel in huge swarms that can destroy a whole season's worth of crops.

The grasshopper itself has to be careful as well. Some if its relatives, such as the mantises, will make a meal out of a grasshopper. Many birds, frogs, and snakes also eat any grasshopper they find. In certain parts of the world, even people eat grasshoppers. Whether they are dried, fried, jellied, roasted, dipped in honey, or ground into **meal**, they can be a good source of **nutrients**.

But grasshoppers have their ways of avoiding danger too. They can smell and hear an enemy, and, of course, they can hop. A grasshopper can hop so well because of its long hind legs. And though grasshoppers usually hop or crawl to get around, most kinds can also fly.

Usually, male grasshoppers are the ones that chirp or sing. They rub their wings together, or they rub their hind legs against their front wings. The song is the male's way of calling the female grasshopper.

LEARN MORE! READ THESE ARTICLES…
ANTS • CRICKETS • INSECTS

Answer: Farmers don't like locusts because they destroy crops.

An Itchy Situation

'**M**-m-m-m-m-m-s-s-z-z-sz-sz-n-n-z-z-zing-ing-ing!'

The humming sound you hear when a mosquito is near your ear comes from the fast beat of the mosquito's wings. Actually, that's the hum of the female mosquito. It is only the female mosquito that bites and leaves those itchy lumps on your arms or legs. The male mosquito seems to be satisfied with a meal of nectar and other plant juices.

Mosquitoes are insects that are usually found wherever the weather is damp or where there are rivers, lakes, or swamps. That's because mosquitoes must lay their eggs in water. Otherwise, the eggs could not hatch. Mosquitoes sometimes lay their eggs in ponds, and other times they lay them in ditches. They will even lay them in tins partly filled with rainwater. When the eggs hatch, the young mosquitoes look like little worms.

Sometimes mosquitoes fly so high up in the air that they even get in through the open windows of tall apartment buildings in big cities. In the far north, near the North Pole, there are so many mosquitoes in summer that when they fly they look like black clouds.

Getting rid of mosquitoes is difficult. One way is to drain all the water out of ditches, swamps, and ponds where they lay their eggs. To destroy full-grown mosquitoes, different kinds of insecticides are used. An insecticide is a powder or liquid for killing harmful insects. Unfortunately, it can be dangerous for animals and people too.

LEARN MORE! READ THESE ARTICLES…
BEES • CRICKETS • INSECTS

SEARCH LIGHT

Find and correct the errors in the following sentence: Mosquitoes live in dry places such as deserts, because they must lay their eggs in sand.

Magnified image of young, newly hatched mosquitoes.
© Science Pictures Limited/Corbis

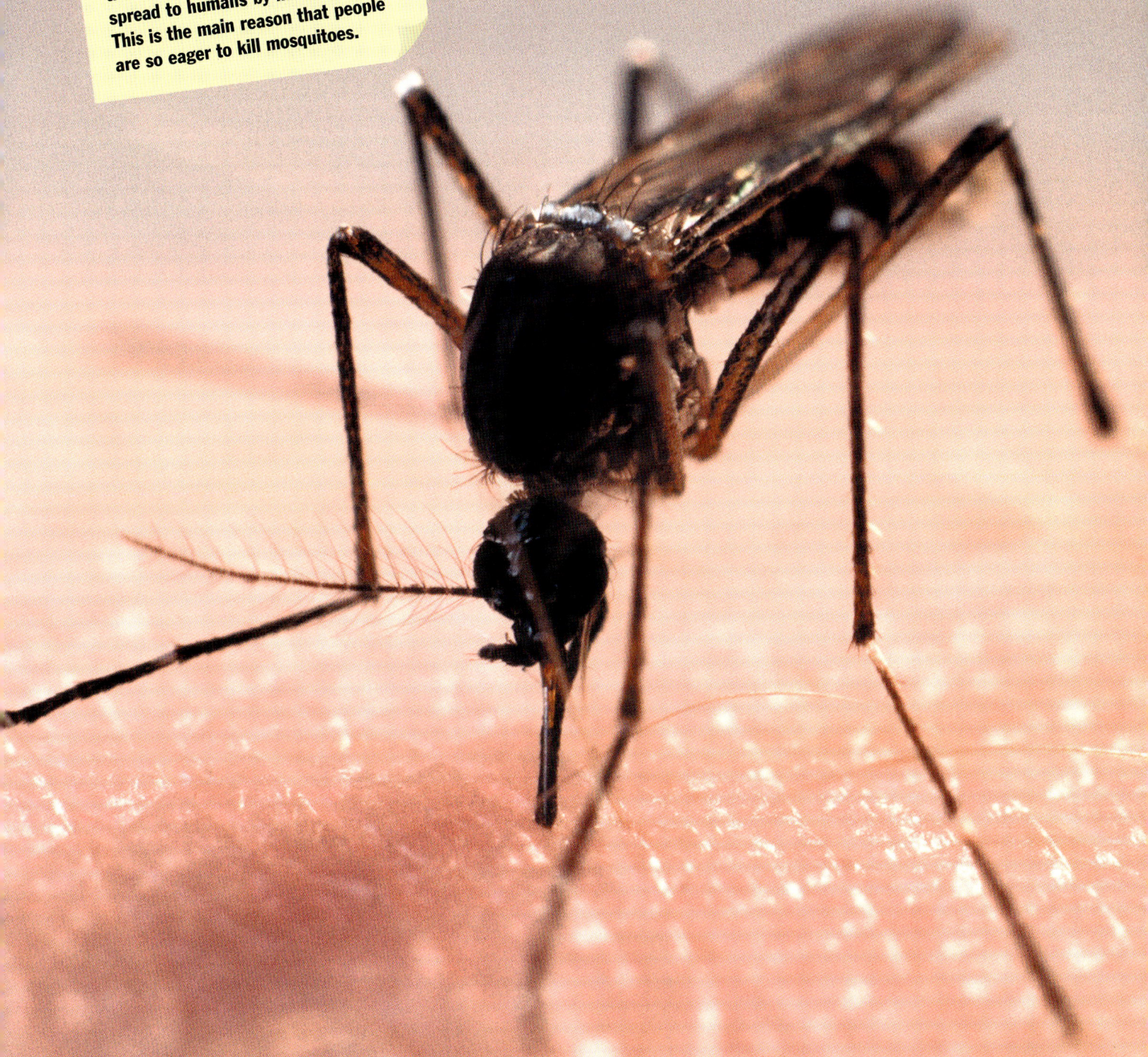

A female mosquito sucks blood from a human arm.

Answer: Mosquitoes live in damp places or near rivers, swamps, and lakes, because they must lay their eggs in water.

47

Majestic American Beasts

The bison, or American buffalo, is the largest land animal in North America. A bull bison stands 2 metres tall at the shoulder and weighs almost a tonne. Bison once roamed the **vast** plains in herds of many thousands of animals. The shaggy bison were looking for fresh fields of tasty grass.

Bison grazing in Wyoming's Yellowstone National Park.
© Darrell Gulin/Corbis

In order to live on the cold Great Plains, the American Indians needed rich food, warm clothing, and strong shelter. The herds of bison gave them all of these things. Bison meat was their daily food. They made warm clothes and blankets from the thick skins. They also used the skins to make **moccasins** and tents. They used the horns to make containers and the bones to make tools.

The Plains Indians killed just enough bison for their needs. The European settlers were different. With their guns they could kill bison in larger numbers than the Indians had with their arrows and spears. Some of the settlers used the bison they killed. But other people killed for sport or just to keep animals from being used by the Indians.

So there came a time when very few bison were left. Animal lovers tried to make people see how important it was to let the bison live. The governments of Canada and the United States finally put all the bison they could find into national parks and other safe places.

There probably will never be millions of bison again, but there are thousands today. There is also a European bison called the 'wisent'. The wisent is even larger than the American bison - and it is even more scarce.

SEARCH LIGHT

The U.S. Army once killed bison to make the Plains Indians surrender. Why would killing bison achieve this? (Hint: What did the Plains Indians get from bison in addition to food?)

LEARN MORE! READ THESE ARTICLES...
CATTLE • EAGLES • HORSES

DID YOU KNOW?
The bison was once so plentiful that it was used on an American coin - the 'buffalo nickel'. On the other side was the head of a Plains Indian.

Answer: The Plains Indians followed the great bison herds as they moved throughout the year. They got their food, tents, clothing, and tools from the animals. When the army killed the bison, they were killing everything the Plains Indians used for survival.

Howling at the Moon

SEARCH LIGHT

Coyotes are
part of
which family?
a) cat
b) dog
c) Jones

Alone coyote howling at the Moon is probably familiar to anyone who's watched cowboy movies. It's true that the coyote is famous for its night concerts. Sometimes it utters short yaps and at other times it makes long howls. This is how coyotes communicate, but to people coyotes sound sad.

The coyote is mostly found in North America. It is sometimes called the 'little wolf' or 'brush wolf'. This is because it is related to the wolf. Both are members of the dog family. But the coyote is smaller than the wolf.

The coyote's fur is long and rough. It is greyish brown in colour, although there is sometimes a patch of white at the throat and belly. The **muzzle** is narrow and has a darker colour. A coyote's legs may be reddish and its tail bushy and black-tipped.

The coyote is most active after dark. It hunts for its food alone or in a group called a 'pack'. It generally feeds on **rodents** and **hares**. A coyote can follow and chase animals for long distances. Sometimes coyotes like to eat vegetables, fruit, and insects.

Coyote roaming the forest.
© Royalty-Free/Corbis

To find a mate, a coyote may travel for miles. The coyote pair, the male and the female, sometimes stay together for life. Both parents look after the pups. The young live with their parents for as long as three years. They help to look after and protect their brothers and sisters that are born after them.

Sometimes coyotes have been hunted and killed to protect farm animals. But they can still be found in many areas where people live.

LEARN MORE! READ THESE ARTICLES…
BISON • DOGS • RABBITS AND HARES

Coyotes are well known for the various sounds they make. At times it appears that they're howling at the Moon.
© Jeff Vanuga/Corbis

51

DID YOU KNOW?
Most people think of the American Wild West when they think of coyotes. But coyotes have been showing up all over the United States. Some have even been seen in New York City.

Answer: b) dog

Cousins of the Dinosaurs

When scientists first found remains of dinosaurs, they thought they had found giant lizards. They later realized that dinosaurs and lizards are different types of animals, but they are related. Both are types of reptiles.

(Top) Komodo dragon; (bottom) gecko.

There are many kinds of lizard. They may be green, grey, red, brown, blue, yellow, black, or almost any colour! Some are longer than a man, and some are so tiny you could hold them between your fingers. The smallest lizards in the world belong to the skink and gecko families. The largest is the Komodo dragon of Southeast Asia.

Most lizards have a long tail, dry scaly skin, strong short legs, and long toes. They also have sharp claws. Some have spiny scales under their toes, which help them cling to rocks or branches.

Draco lizards are also called the 'flying lizards'. They can't fly the way a bird does, but they have a tough skin that can spread out. They can jump from a tree and sail a long way through the air.

A little lizard called the 'American chameleon' is pretty and friendly. These tiny creatures are helpful to humans because they eat harmful insects. They seem to be able to change colour when they want to. They can't really do that, but their skins do change from brown to green when there are changes in light and temperature.

The Gila monster is one of the few lizards that are dangerous. It is black and pink or orange, which makes it easy to see. And that's a good thing because the Gila has a poisonous bite.

SEARCH LIGHT

True or false? The flying lizard doesn't really fly.

LEARN MORE! READ THESE ARTICLES…
BIRDS • INSECTS • SNAKES

DID YOU KNOW?
If another animal tries to eat the glass lizard by grabbing its tail, the tail comes off. The other animal may then think it has caught the whole lizard.

The five-lined skink is very small. It usually grows to be only about 13 to 20 centimetres long.

Answer: TRUE. It jumps and glides through the air.

SEARCH LIGHT

Most monkeys live in
a) the Himalayas.
b) hot deserts.
c) tropical rainforests.

Cute Clowns and Big Bullies

Visitors to a zoo are always attracted by the **antics** of monkeys. Many animals have tails. But none use them in as many ways as monkeys do. And no monkey uses its tail as cleverly as the spider monkey.

(Top) Family of baboons in Tanzania, Africa; (bottom) Central American spider monkey sitting on a tree branch.

The furry spider monkey is the champion **acrobat** of the monkey world. Its long arms help it to swing through trees. Its tail is thin, long, and very strong. It can reach almost all the way around a thick tree trunk. The tail holds onto the tree like a hand, although it doesn't have fingers.

Monkeys can be as small as kittens. The spider monkey is small, but the tiny playful marmoset is smaller - sometimes no larger than a mouse. Howler monkeys arc quite big, about as big as a medium-sized dog. And their howl is so loud that they can be heard for miles. These monkeys **roam** through the trees in groups looking for food. Baboons are among the largest of all monkeys. They have dog-like snouts and large sharp teeth. They like to fight each other to see which is the strongest. The winner becomes the leader of the group.

Most monkeys feed mainly on fruits, flowers, and seeds. Some include insects and eggs in their diet. Baboons sometimes eat small mammals. Baboons live in the dry grasslands of Africa. And some macaques live in the Himalayas. But most monkeys live in warm places with lots of trees, such as tropical rainforests.

Monkeys often share their habitat with their close relatives the apes. And though apes are brainier, monkeys have a bonus too: they have tails and apes don't.

LEARN MORE! READ THESE ARTICLES...
CATS · DOGS · PARROTS AND COCKATOOS

Patas monkeys like this one live in bands in the grass and scrub regions of Central America.
© Kennan Ward/Corbis

Answer: c) tropical rainforests.

DID YOU KNOW?
Rabbits that live in hot areas usually have bigger ears than those that live in cold areas. Larger ears help animals stay cool, while smaller ears help animals keep from getting too cold.

Long Ears
and Strong Legs

If you see an animal outside that hops and has long ears, it could be a rabbit or a hare. Rabbits have tails that are white on the bottom. That's why some American rabbits are called 'cottontails'. Hares have longer ears and longer legs than rabbits.

European rabbits are the ancestors of all **domestic** rabbits worldwide. Rabbits live together in underground **burrows** called 'warrens'. Inside the warren a mother rabbit carefully shreds leaves and collects grass to line a nest for her babies. Then she pulls bits of fur from her thick coat to make a warm and snug bed. Baby rabbits haven't any fur at first, so the mother must keep them warm.

The nest is usually deep enough in the warren to keep the babies safe. But when a rabbit sees a **predator** looking for the nest, the rabbit will thump its back legs to warn other rabbits. Rabbit mothers aren't gentle when their babies are in danger from dogs, foxes, snakes, owls, or hawks. They bite and kick hard with their feet!

Hares don't build warrens. Their homes are shallow holes that they dig in the grass, under trees, or in brush heaps. Some hares in cold climates have a white coat during the winter and a brown one in the summer.

Both rabbits and hares love to eat green plants such as clover as well as the bark, buds, and berries of trees and shrubs. They search for food from sundown to dawn and then hide during the day. And if you've heard the story about a rabbit jumping into a thorny bush to stay safe - it's true. Rabbits make twisting paths through thorny underbrush, where their enemies can't follow.

Cute and cuddly pet rabbit.
© Kelly-Mooney Photography/Corbis

SEARCH LIGHT

Fill in the gap: Rabbits have a tail that is _____ on the bottom.

LEARN MORE! READ THESE ARTICLES...
COYOTES • DOGS • OWLS

The American black-tailed jackrabbit is actually a hare. It's easily recognized by its long ears tipped with black colouring.
© Darrell Gulin/Corbis

Answer: Rabbits have a tail that is white on the bottom.

SEARCH LIGHT

Why do you suppose raccoons are sometimes called 'bandits'?

Masked Bandits

The raccoon is a smart and curious animal, easily recognized by the black mask across its eyes and the black bands ringing its bushy tail. These bands give the raccoon its nickname, 'ringtail'.

To many people in North and South America raccoons are animals that dig through rubbish during the night at campsites and in town rubbish bins. They're **nocturnal** animals, sleeping in the daytime, and they eat many different kinds of foods. Raccoons often search in shallow water for food such as frogs and crayfish, and this once caused people to believe that raccoons washed their food.

Raccoons' bodies usually measure 50 to 66 centimetres long, and their tails are about 30 centimetres long. They weigh about 10 kilos, though a large male may weigh more than twice that amount. A raccoon's **forefeet** look like slender human hands, and the creature can handle objects quickly and easily.

A raccoon at a pond.
© D. Robert & Lorri Franz/Corbis

Raccoons range from northern Alberta, in Canada, through most of the United States and into South America. They like wooded areas near water, but many also live in cities. They swim and climb, and they often live together high in hollow trees, in openings in rocks, in tree stumps, or in other animals' burrows. In cities they are often found living in the attics of houses.

In spring a female raccoon usually has three or four babies. When they are 10 or 11 weeks old, the mother starts taking them on short outings. The young stay with their mother for about a year.

Raccoons are considered pests in some areas, and in the eastern United States they are the primary carrier of the disease **rabies**.

LEARN MORE! READ THESE ARTICLES...
COYOTES • PIGS • RABBITS AND HARES

Raccoons that are used to being around people may seem so friendly and cute that you want to pick them up. Don't! They're still wild animals with sharp teeth, and they may carry diseases.
© Joe McDonald/Corbis

Answer: They are called bandits because they look like they are wearing masks and because they steal food from rubbish bins.

Legless Wonders

(Top) Ghost corn snake; **(bottom)** woma python.

Aside from worms, almost every animal you see on land has legs. But snakes are different. They don't have legs, or arms either. Most snakes move around by pushing against the ground, scraping it with their tough scales.

Snakes look slippery and slimy, but they're not. Their skin actually feels like cool soft leather. As a snake gets bigger, its skin gets tighter and tighter until the snake wiggles right out of it, wearing a new skin. A snake sheds its skin this way a few times a year.

The smallest snakes are no larger than worms. All snakes are hunters, though. Small snakes eat insects. Larger snakes eat rats or squirrels or rabbits. The huge pythons and anacondas can swallow a deer.

Some snakes use poison called 'venom' to catch animals. They deliver their poison with a bite. Others are constrictors, which means that they wrap themselves around their prey and suffocate it. Still other snakes eat bird eggs. Snakes swallow their food whole, without chewing. The jaws may be hinged so that the snake can eat something larger than its own head. A snake that has just eaten may not need another meal for days and days.

Snakes are eaten by big birds such as eagles, hawks, and owls. The Indian mongoose (a mammal) kills cobras. Wild hogs stamp on snakes to kill them. And, of course, many people kill snakes on sight.

Most snakes avoid people and won't hurt you if you don't bother them. Still, it's a good idea to leave wild snakes alone.

SEARCH LIGHT

True or false? Snakes chew their food.

LEARN MORE! READ THESE ARTICLES...
BIRDS • LIZARDS • PIGS

The sea snake has a flat tail that it can use like an oar to move itself through the water.
© Brandon D. Cole/Corbis

Answer: FALSE. Snakes swallow their food whole.

G L O S S A R Y

abdomen in insects, the end portion of the body that is behind the head and thorax (middle section)

acrobat performer who does tricks and physical routines that require strength, balance, and body control, often above the ground

antenna (plural: antennae) in biology, a slender organ on the head of some insects and crustaceans (such as shrimps and lobsters) that allows them to sense their environment

antics playful or funny actions

bovine animal group that includes cattle, oxen, bison, and buffalo

bray to make a sound like the loud harsh call of a donkey

burden weight or load to carry

burrow deep hole or tunnel made in the ground by an animal for shelter

bushman in Australia, a person who lives in the bush (wilderness)

contour the outline of a figure, body, or surface

crest (adjective: crested) 1) in biology, a standing clump of fur or feathers, usually on an animal's head; 2) in geography, the upper edge or limit of something, such as the top of a mountain

crossbreed to produce offspring from parents of two varieties or species

digestive system parts of the body that work together to break down food into simpler forms that can be used by the body

domestic (verb: domesticate) tame

dual two

echo to repeat or imitate a sound

forefeet (singular: forefoot) the front feet of an animal with four or more feet

hare rabbit-like animal

impish playfully naughty

instinct natural tendency of a living thing to respond in a particular way to a situation

litter group of newborn animals born to the same mother at the same time

majestic grand or splendid

meal coarsely ground substance

moccasin soft leather shoe first worn by Native American Indians

muzzle animal's snout (jaw and nose)

nectar sweet liquid produced by plants and used by bees in making honey

nocturnal active at night

nutrient substance that a living thing needs in order to stay healthy and grow

parasite creature that lives on another, which it usually injures

pest plant or animal that is annoying or destructive

pollen (verb: pollinate) very fine dusty substance that comes from flowers; it is important in the reproduction of other plants

polo team sport played by hitting a wooden ball with mallets through goalposts while on horseback

predator (adjective: predatory) animal that lives by eating other animals

prey an animal eaten by another animal

pygmy something very small for its kind

rabies serious disease of animals that is usually passed on through the bite of a sick (rabid) animal; its effects include extreme salivation, strange behaviour, and usually death

roam to travel or wander freely through a wide area

rodent major animal group that includes mice, squirrels, and other small gnawing animals

sacred holy

shears cutting device similar to scissors but usually larger

stationary unmoving

superstition unproven belief usually based on a mistaken idea of how something is caused

temperament personality or usual mood

thorax the middle of the three main divisions of the body of an insect

tropical having to do with the Earth's warmest and most humid (moist) climates

tusk long tooth that overhangs when the mouth is closed and serves for digging food or as a weapon

unique very unusual or one-of-a-kind

vast huge or spacious

vegetarian person or animal that does not eat meat

veterinarian doctor who takes care of animals

vibrate to move rapidly back and forth or from side to side

warm-blooded having a body temperature that stays mostly unchanged and is not affected by the surrounding environment

waterproof not affected by water

weaned capable of and used to eating food rather than nursing

I N D E X